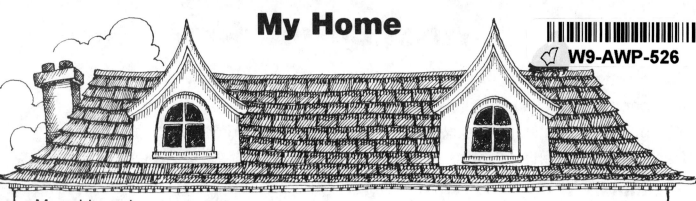

My Home

My address is:

Street _____

Town _____

Province _____

Country _____

Postal Code _____

Continent _____

Planet _____

My telephone number is:

_____

My area code is:

_____

In my home there are _____ rooms.

My favourite room is _____

because _____

In my home there are _____ windows.

My favourite window is _____

because _____

What Do You Say?

There are many words that can be used in sentences to show
that people are talking.
When you write a story, you can use these different words.
Replace the underlined words in these sentences.

Example:

"Run!" _____said_____ the man.

"Run!" _____yelled_____ the man.

"Run!" _____screamed_____ the man.

She _____chatted_____ with the chimpanzee.

She _____ with the chimpanzee.

She _____ with the chimpanzee.

He _____talked_____ to a tiger.

He _____ to a tiger.

He _____ to a tiger.

They _____conversed_____ with a polar bear.

They _____ with a polar bear.

They _____ with a polar bear.

We _____spoke_____ to a rhinoceros.

We _____ to a rhinoceros.

We _____ to a rhinoceros.

They _____conferred_____ with their furry friends.

They _____ with their furry friends.

They _____ with their furry friends.

Everyone _____discussed_____ the problem.

Everyone _____ the problem.

Everyone _____ the problem.

The animals _____grunted_____ when they saw the people.

The animals _____ when they saw the people.

The animals _____ when they saw the people.

The animals _____squeaked_____ at the crowds.

The animals _____ at the crowds.

The animals _____ at the crowds.

The zoo keeper _____roared_____ at the animals.

The zoo keeper _____ at the animals.

The zoo keeper _____ at the animals.

Animal School

The song "Talk to the Animals" says that we could learn a lot from animals
if we could speak their languages.
What could these animals teach people to do?

A chimp could teach _____

because _____

A tiger could teach _____

because _____

A cheetah could teach _____

because _____

An elephant could teach _____

because _____

An eagle could teach _____

because _____

A buffalo could teach _____

because _____

A polar bear could teach _____

because _____

A kangaroo could teach _____

because _____

Can you speak rhinoceros? Of courseros.
Can't you?

Bibbedy Bobbidy Boo

Some words in stories, such as these from "What's So Funny, Ketu?", are just sounds that are spelled out.
Match the "sound words" with the actions they stand for.

The dog slinked off.	kao, kao, kao!
Nyaloti patted the baby.	prada, prada, prada!
The mosquito buzzed.	tu-e, tu-e, tu-e!
Ketu laughed.	pah, pah, pah!
The dog yelped.	zeee!
Ketu laughed.	ge-e, ge-e, ge-e!
The baby cried.	GU-MAPP!
Ketu rolled out of bed.	kye, kye, kye!
Ketu exploded with laughter.	nun-tun, nun-tun!
The rat leaped onto the bed.	KWAM!
The cow galloped around the tree.	ke-yaa, ke-yaa, ke-yaa!
Ketu fell over dead.	TWUM!

Ketu's Play

There are six pictures with the story "What's So Funny, Ketu?".
Someone is speaking in each picture.
Write the words these people might be saying.

Look at the picture on page 11. What do you think Ketu might be saying?

Ketu: _____

_____

_____

Look at the picture on page 13. What do you think Nyaloti might be saying?

Nyaloti: _____

_____

_____

Look at the picture on page 15. What do you think Ketu might be saying?

Ketu: _____

_____

_____

Look at the picture on page 17. What do you think Nyaloti might be saying?

Nyaloti: _____

_____

_____

Look at the picture on page 19. What do you think the chief might be saying?

Chief: _____

_____

_____

Look at the picture on page 21. What do you think the baby might be saying?

Baby: _____

_____

_____

Building with "le"

Many words with two sounds have a letter plus "le" as the second sound.
Complete the "le" words in these sentences.

Example:

A dog with long ears could be a b _eagle_.

An a_____ a day keeps the doctor away.

She has a d_____ in her cheek.

The easy work was too s_____

The baby bottle has a n_____ on top.

The rain made a big mud p_____

A violin is also called a f_____

He had a b_____ bath.

The soldiers fought a large b_____

The child bought a b_____ of soda pop.

We like to play with the jigsaw p_____

The dangerous dog wore a m_____ on his face.

Write four more "le" words.

_____le _____le _____le _____le

Valentines for Everyone

In the story "One Zillion Valentines," Milton and Marvin are always disagreeing with each other. Complete the second part of each of these arguments.

"If I had a lot of money, I'd buy all those valentines."

"That's silly. You _____

"No one ever sent me a valentine."

"That's because _____

"I never have any money."

"You _____

"I bet we could make a zillion valentines."

"A zillion _____

"Now what do we do?"

"We _____

"We'll need a zillion stamps."

"No _____

"I guess we made too many."

"No _____

"But I bet we don't get a valentine from anyone."

"Sure we do. _____

Valentines

Make as many words as you can using the letters in the word "VALENTINES".

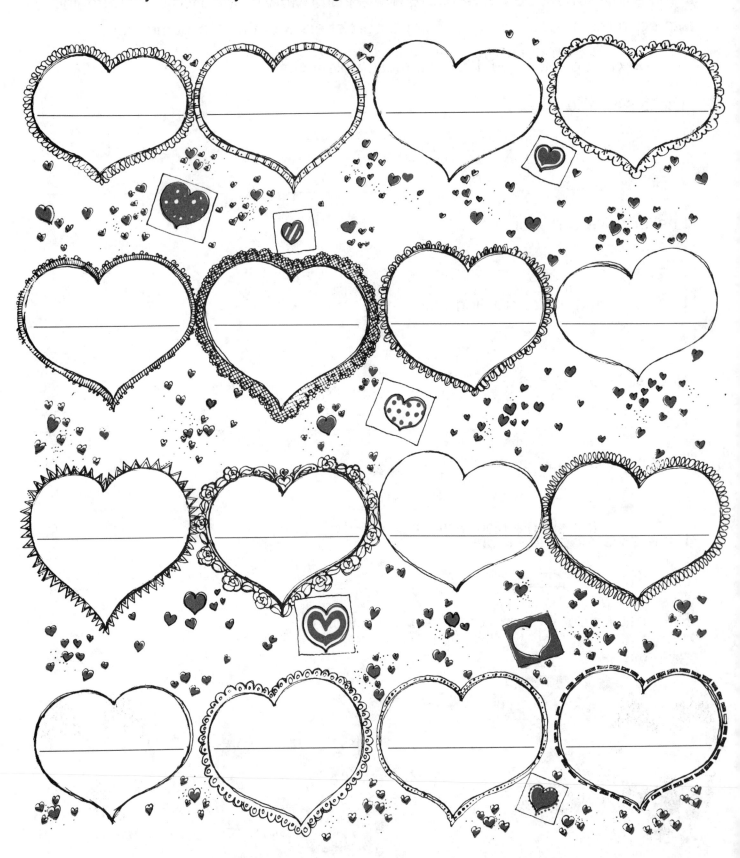

A Valentine Poem

Use the pattern of the poem "Lavender's Blue" to write a Valentine's Day poem.

Lavender's blue, dilly, dilly, lavender's green,

_____, dilly, dilly,

_____

Who told you so, dilly, dilly, who told you so?

_____, dilly, dilly,

_____

Call up your men, dilly, dilly, set them to work,

_____, dilly, dilly,

_____

Some to make hay, dilly, dilly, some to thresh corn,

_____, dilly, dilly,

_____

If it should hap, dilly, dilly, if it should chance,

_____, dilly, dilly,

_____

Lavender's blue, dilly, dilly, lavender's green,

_____, dilly, dilly

_____

Story Period!

Make this story easier to read.
Place a period at the end of each sentence.

One October day a Hen looked out her window she saw an apple tree
growing in her backyard she did not remember seeing a tree there
the day before the tree said that some trees grow fast the Hen said
she had never seen a tree that had ten furry toes the tree said
that some of them do then the Hen said she had never seen a tree
with two long pointed ears the tree said that some trees have them
the Hen said she had never seen a tree speak from a mouth
full of sharp teeth the tree said some of them can the Hen said
that some trees lose all of their leaves the tree began to quiver
and shake all the leaves dropped off the Hen saw a Wolf standing
where the tree had been she locked her shutters and closed her windows
it is always difficult to pretend to be something you are not..

Double or Not

The last letter of these words is doubled before adding "ed" or "ing".
Add "ed" or "ing" to each word.

slam_____   split_____

stop_____   drop_____

slip_____   mop_____

run_____   win_____

grab_____   knit_____

hop_____   can_____

begin_____   drip_____

Use four of the words you made in sentences.

1. _____

_____

2. _____

_____

3. _____

_____

4. _____

_____

The Son's Story

Write the story "The Elephant and His Son" as if the son
is telling a friend what happened.

_____

_____

_____

_____

_____

_____

_____

_____

_____

_____

_____

_____

Moral: Adults may know more,
        but children can still see what is happening.

To Add or Not to Add

Adding "ing" or "ed" to words can be tricky. Sometimes you have to double the last letter and sometimes you don't.
Add "ing" or "ed" to each word below and then print the word in the correct list.

begin_____   stop_____   look_____   pop_____

ask_____   tell_____   run_____   send_____

end_____   bend_____   hop_____   stand_____

slip_____   grab_____   hit_____   sell_____

Double the last letter.   Do not double the last letter.

_____   _____

_____   _____

_____   _____

_____   _____

_____   _____

_____   _____

I Want to Crow

Add the missing words to retell the story "The Young Rooster."

A young Rooster _____ summoned to his _____ bedside.

"Son, my _____ has come to _____ end,"

said the _____ bird. "Now it _____ your turn

to _____ up the morning _____ each day.

Early _____ next day, the _____ Rooster

flew up _____ the roof of _____ barn.

He stood _____ facing the east.

"_____ have never done _____ before,"

said the _____ Rooster. "I must _____ my best."

He _____ his head and _____

He made a _____ noise. The sun _____ not come up.

"_____ is a disaster!" _____ the Pig.

"We _____ our sunshine!" shouted _____ Sheep.

"Rooster you _____ crow much louder," _____ a Bull.

The _____ morning, the young _____ flew up

to _____ roof of the _____ again.

He took _____ deep breath, he _____ back

his head, _____ crowed a loud _____

He saw the _____ of the morning _____ coming up

over _____ trees.

You may _____ at first, but _____ you may succeed.

16

Almost the Same

Print each word from the list beside a word below that means almost the same thing.

youngster   Father   aged
rooster   morning   drizzle
covered   louder   summoned
beginning   trees   ache
job   animals

beasts _____

pain _____

noisier _____

called _____

dawn _____

old _____

blanketed _____

start _____

work _____

child _____

chicken _____

Dad _____

forest _____

rain _____

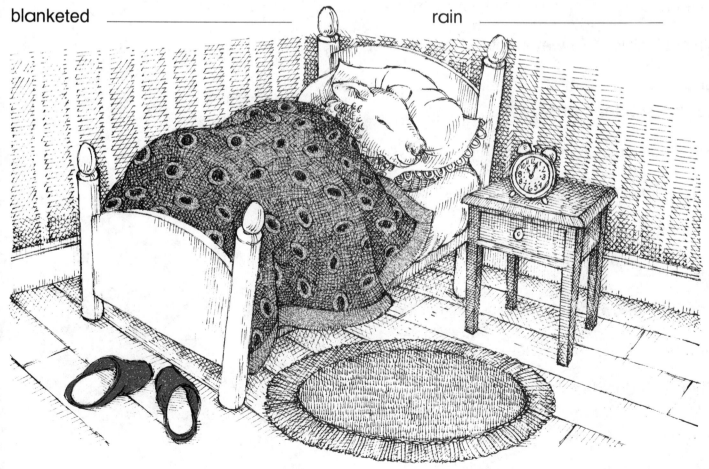

Mighty Words

Complete these sentences using information from "Mightiest of Them All."

Once there was and twice there wasn't, a _____,

a _____, a little _____

She was born under drooping, snow-laden branches of some _____

She first looked out when the last big snow had emptied the _____

In one bound she was off and _____;

in another she was in the open _____;

in another she was in the soft, powdery _____

She cried out, "Tell me, Snow, are you _____
The Snow said, "If I were, the Chinook Wind could not breathe on me

and melt me to _____

She cried out, "Tell me, Wind, are you _____

Chinook said, "If I were, how could the mountains _____ me

and _____ me and _____ me

out through the narrow pass?"

She cried out, "Tell me, Mountain, are you _____

Mountain said, "If I were, how could the earth make me _____,

make me _____, _____ me up

and _____ me low?"

The little snowshoe hare also asked the _____

and the _____

Then she decided that she was _____

_____

18

Words in the Snow

Can you find the twelve words that the little snowshoe hare has hidden?
Each word ends in "s" or "es".

e	c	a	s	t	l	e	s
g	f	r	i	e	n	d	s
g	r	a	s	s	e	s	b
s	u	s	d	s	x	x	r
p	x	e	i	e	x	x	a
a	b	u	s	h	e	s	n
t	x	x	h	s	x	s	c
c	x	x	e	a	e	x	h
h	p	a	s	s	e	s	e
e	x	b	o	x	e	s	s
s	x	m	i	x	e	s	x

In Other Words

These expressions are from the story "Mightiest of Them All."
Write another way of saying the same thing.

once there was, and twice there wasn't

_____

under the snow-laden branches of some saplings

_____

when the last of the big snow had emptied the sky

_____

sunk in the soft, powdery snow, high over her haunches, deep up to her ears

_____

Are you the mightiest of them all?

_____

melt me to nothingness

_____

the sun's fiery ball sinks to rest

_____

mountain, you tip the sky and pierce the clouds

_____

More Than One

To make a word mean more than one, you usually add "s" or "es".
Change the words below to make them mean more than one.

rabbit_____   mix_____

fox_____   guess_____

ash_____   box_____

branch_____   night_____

friend_____   splash_____

mountain_____   bench_____

colour_____   dress_____

egg_____   dish_____

leg_____   match_____

patch_____   king_____

home_____   bush_____

grass_____   castle_____

A Dog and Wolf Fight

Answer these questions about the story "A War Between the Dog and the Wolf."

What did the dog and the wolf do when they met under the oak tree?

_____

_____

What news was the wolf interested in?

_____

_____

What promise had the wolf made to the dog?

_____

_____

What did the dog mean when he said, "But I will hear you,"?

_____

_____

Why was the dog loyal to his master?

_____

_____

How were the little piglets saved the first time?

_____

_____

Why was the wolf angry?

_____

_____

What did the wolf threaten to do?

_____

_____

Who was in the wolf's army?

_____

_____

Who was in the dog's army?

_____

_____

Why did the dog win?

_____

_____

Who Said What?

Who said these lines in the story "A War Between the Dog and the Wolf"?

"Listen, my friend, I hear that your master's pig just had a litter of piglets,"

said _____

"The bomb they threw blew my tail right off,"

said _____

"I lost part of my tail,"

cried _____

"I am in very bad trouble and you won't be able to help me,"

answered _____

"Have you forgotten your friend?"

whispered _____

"Promise me you will not give me away,"

said _____

"Pssst! Come here,"

whispered _____

"Very well, I shall be there when you need me,"

said _____

What a Definition!

Write a definition for each of these words from "A War Between the Dog and the Wolf."

litter _____

piglet _____

master _____

disloyal _____

barnyard _____

chorus _____

limped _____

howl _____

thud _____

traitor _____

declare war _____

loped _____

boar _____

gander _____

drake _____

How Do I Marco Polo?

Sometimes we use words that mean one thing to mean something else.
For example, "Let's all bugaloo!" could mean "Let's all dance!"

What do you think these expressions could mean?
Rumplestiltskin, children!

_____

Let's all Mowgli.

_____

Kublai Khan, my people!

_____

Marco Polo, everyone.

_____

Robin Hood, boys and girls!

_____

Superman, everybody!

_____

Let's all Miss Piggy!

_____

Story Time

Sometimes, a story has certain words in it
that help you decide what kind of story it is.

What kind of story do each of these sentences make you think of?
Example:
Once upon a time
fairy tale

The elephant said, "I can fly, too!"

_____

The star grew brighter and brighter.

_____

The monster turned and looked at the child.

_____

And then I woke up!

_____

The cellar was dark and damp.

_____

The raft bobbed up and down on the river.

_____

They all lived happily ever after.

_____

Rain, Rain, Come Again

Use your own words to describe each of the following things which are found in the poem "Bringing the Rain to Kapiti Plain."

This is the great Kapiti Plain

_____

_____

This is the cloud

_____

_____

This is the grass

_____

_____

These are the cows

_____

_____

This is Ki-pat

_____

_____

This is the eagle

_____

_____

This is the feather

_____

_____

This is the arrow

_____

_____

This is the bow

_____

_____

This was the shot

_____

_____

Building Poems

"Bringing the Rain to Kapiti Plain" follows a pattern.
Use the same pattern to write your own poem.

This Is the Sun

This is the sun that nobody sees.

This is the _____

that covers the sun that nobody sees.

This is the _____

that _____

that covers the sun that nobody sees.

This is the _____

that _____

that _____

that covers the sun that nobody sees.

This is the _____

that _____

that _____

that _____

that no longer covers the sun that everyone now sees.

Words Drop Like Rain

There are two letters underlined in each of the words in the clouds.
Under each of these words print the list words that have the same sound
spelled the same way.

joy	team	hay	plain	tray	head	real
leather	afraid	bread	air	meat	weather	wheat
may	stain	boy	sea	thread	pain	trail
meadow	stay	play	main	dream	steady	

beam

feather

rain

away

The Warning Fire

Number the sentences in the correct order to tell the story "Kenji Moto the Hermit."

( )   Kenji paused for a moment's rest and gazed out toward the ocean.

( )   "How did the fire get started?" asked a villager.

( )   Each of them promised there would always be a place in his new home for Kenji Moto the hermit.

( )   "Why don't they hurry? The big wave is almost here."

( )   He tilled a small rice field for food and to trade for fish.

( )   Kenji looked in wonderment, trying to understand what was happening.

( )   The ocean seemed to be rising up to engulf the sky.

( )   As they climbed higher, they were able to see the wall of water.

( )   They realized that Kenji had deliberately set fire to his field.

( )   "A fire! A fire would be seen from far away."

( )   "With this," said Kenji, holding up the smoking torch.

( )   Desperately, he looked around for some way to send a warning.

( )   Many years ago, the entire village had been swept away.

( )   The villagers were mostly fishermen, making a living from the ocean.

Find Another Way

These sentences are from the story "Kenji Moto the Hermit."
Write another way of saying the underlined expressions.

Kenji was a hermit <u>by choice</u>.

_____

Kenji could see <u>the village of his birth</u>.

_____

He <u>paused for a moment's rest</u>.

_____

The sky above the ocean <u>was threateningly dark</u>.

_____

The entire village <u>had been swept away</u> by the big wave.

_____

The tidal wave <u>would be upon them</u>.

_____

Then, <u>an idea came to him</u>.

_____

All the villagers <u>were hastening toward the top of the hill</u>.

_____

Words Ahoy!

Each boat carries a cargo of words with a "c" sound or a "g" sound.
Print the words from the cargo list in the correct boat.

Cargo List

magic	signal	face	cover
get	prince	giant	come
huge	gun	car	race
catch	police	hug	edge
give	decide	village	stick
gazed	strange	choice	could
rage	engulf	glance	call

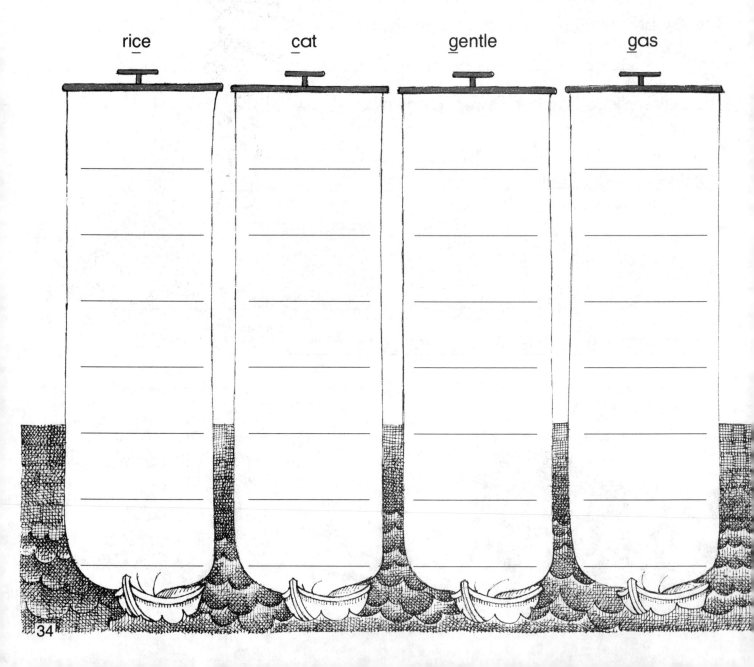

ri<u>c</u>e   <u>c</u>at   <u>g</u>entle   <u>g</u>as

The Huge Puzzle

Complete the crossword puzzle.

ACROSS

2. exercise room at school
4. a small town
6. a kind of hat
9. what you see in a mirror
10. very, very large
11. run to win
12. a two wheeler

DOWN

1. people who protect us
3. pulling a rabbit from a hat
5. a large person
7. the son of a king
8. to make up your mind
9. eaten with chopsticks
10. to go fast

A Special Treasure

Complete these sentences about the story "The Proud King and the Stubborn Duke."

The king and the duke were both _____

_____

The king decided to attack the duke's castle because _____

_____

The country folk promised to help the duke because _____

_____

The duke's people prepared for battle by _____

_____

The king was ready for battle with his _____

_____

The duke's people began to complain because _____

_____

They were worried about the village crops because _____

_____

The women began to mourn because _____

_____

The duke's wife sent a message to the king asking _____

_____

The dearest treasure of each woman was _____

_____

Three, Four or More

Look in the wordsearch to find out how to make each of the list words mean more than one. Circle the word in the word search, and then print it beside the list word.

k	x	x	w	i	v	e	s
n	x	x	x	x	x	x	r
i	l	e	a	v	e	s	e
v	c	x	w	x	e	x	e
e	x	a	o	v	x	x	f
s	h	e	l	v	e	s	s
l	x	a	v	v	x	x	x
i	h	x	e	x	e	x	x
v	x	x	s	x	x	s	x
e	c	h	i	e	f	s	x
s	e	l	v	e	s	x	x

wife _____

wolf _____

leaf _____

self _____

knife _____

calf _____

chief _____

shelf _____

life _____

reef _____

half _____

37

Growing Sentences

Add words to these sentences to make them more interesting.

The king was proud.

The king, _____, was proud.

The king, _____, was proud

because _____

The duke was busy.

In _____,

the duke was busy.

In _____,

the duke, who _____,
was busy.

In _____,

the duke, who _____,

was busy because _____

The food grew less and less.

The food in _____
grew less and less.

The food in _____

grew less and less because _____

When _____ ,

the food in _____

grew less and less because _____

The women came out.

When _____ ,
the women came out.

When _____ ,

the women, who _____ ,
came out.

When _____ ,

the women, who _____ ,

came out because _____

Two Cinderellas

You have probably read or seen the story "Cinderella" when you were younger. Compare that story to "The Indian Cinderella."

	Cinderella	The Indian Cinderella
People	_____	_____
	_____	_____
	_____	_____
	_____	_____
Setting	_____	_____
	_____	_____
	_____	_____
Beginning	_____	_____
	_____	_____
	_____	_____

	Cinderella	The Indian Cinderella
Magic	_____	_____
	_____	_____
	_____	_____
	_____	_____
Ending	_____	_____
	_____	_____
	_____	_____
Different Words	_____	_____
	_____	_____
	_____	_____
	_____	_____

I liked _____ better because

_____

_____

_____

What Comes Next?

Add the missing words to retell the story "The Indian Cinderella."

Once upon a _____, there dwelt a _____ Indian Chief.

He _____ make himself invisible. _____ called him

Strong _____ the Invisible.

Strong _____ lived with his _____ in a tent

_____ the ocean. Many _____ wanted

to marry _____. They knew he _____ marry

the first _____ who could see _____.

Strong Wind's sister _____ ask a maiden _____

she could see _____. If she said _____,

the sister would _____ how he was _____

his sled. If _____ maiden said with _____ pole

or a _____, the sister knew _____ was lying.

One _____ the youngest daughter _____ a great chief

_____ the test. She _____ Strong Wind

was _____ his sled with _____ rainbow.

The sister _____ the girl could _____ Strong Wind.

She _____ Strong Wind's wife.

42

Short Form Fun

An abbreviation is the short way of writing a word.
For example, Van. is the abbreviation for Vancouver.
Draw a line from each word to its abbreviation.

Manager	T.V.
Doctor	St.
Street	Mgr.
government	Dr.
Mister	gov't
North East	Ave.
Canada	Mr.
television	Rev.
Fahrenheit	Fri.
Police Department	Can.
Reverend	Mar.
Avenue	F.
minute	h
hour	P.D.
March	min
Friday	N.E.

May I see the manager, please?

Mgr.

My World and Your World

Write a new song by using the pattern of the song "This Land Is Your Land."

This world is your world
This world is my world.

From _____

      (your city)

To _____

      (a city where a friend or relative lives)

From _____

      (a place in the north of Canada)

To _____

      (a place in the south you have heard about)

This world was made for you and me.

As I was walking

_____

(a street you walk on)

I saw above me

_____

(something wonderful you could see)

I saw below me

_____

(a dream place)

This world was made for you and me.

44

Say It Again

Can you think of another way of saying these words and expressions
from the song "This Land Is Your Land"?

land _____

island _____

lake _____

endless skyway _____

golden _____

ribbon of highway _____

you and me _____

below _____

roamed _____

forests _____

fir-clad _____

mighty _____

a voice was sounding _____

I followed my footsteps _____

A World Puzzle

Can you answer these country questions?

a country that has the same name as a bird you can eat

_____

a country that has the same number of letters in its name as Canada

_____

a country that has two words in its name

_____   _____

a country that is surrounded by water

_____

a country that is smaller than Canada

_____

a country that is bigger than Canada

_____

a country that has deserts

_____

a country that has mountains

_____

a country that someone I know is from

_____

a country I would like to visit

_____

A Peddler's Story

Complete this page using information from "The Piney Woods Peddler."

Once, back a ways, a peddler travelled around.

His job was _____

His daughter asked for one thing:

_____

So, he traded his big black horse

for _____

He traded the _____

for _____

He traded the _____

for _____

He traded the _____

for _____

He traded the _____

for _____

Was he satisfied with the dime? Why?

_____

_____

The Snake and the Stick

The story "The Piney Woods Peddler" includes a tall tale about a rattlesnake.
Imagine that you are a storyteller, and write that part of the story
as you would tell it.

_____

_____

_____

_____

_____

_____

_____

_____

_____

_____

_____

_____

The Same Beginnings

To make his story sound interesting, the author of "The Piney Woods Peddler" sometimes used groups of words that start with the same letter.

What words did the author use instead of the following?

Example:

an Evergreen Woods peddler

a Piney Woods peddler

a bright silver dollar

_____

my lovely sweet daughter

_____

ging dang waddle

_____

bees were a-humming

_____

He jumped on his horse.

_____

large brown cow

_____

The woodpeckers were a-digging.

_____

Opposites Attract

Use an opposite to complete each pair.

up and _____

wrong from _____

near and _____

man and _____

big or _____

the sky and the _____

buying and _____

sons and _____

come and _____

shiny or _____

singing or _____.

rich or _____

cow and _____

Filling Out a Report

In the story "Ida's Idea," something was missing each day.
Imagine that you are Ida, and fill out this report for a detective.

Missing Things Report

Name: Ida _____

Address: _____

Missing Object: _____

Description: _____

_____

Where Object
Came From: _____

_____

Last Place
Object Was Seen: _____

_____

Why Object Was
Important: _____

_____

Evidence: _____

_____

What You Think
Happened: _____

_____

Signed _____

A Word Wonderland

Add the endings at the top of the chart to the words. Watch out!
Before you add the ending, check the last letter of the word.
(You will not be able to add all the endings to every word.)

	ing	er	ed
nibble	nibbling		
come			
plan			
fight			
bike			
hop			
smile			
shine			
race			
look			
swim			
skate			
bike			
use			

Ida's Home

Draw a plan of Ida and her mother's home.
Include rooms, furniture, appliances, and special things that they own.

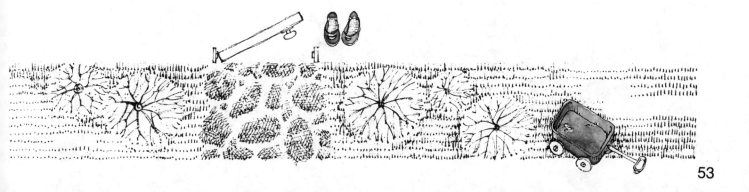

New Words from Old

Make new words by adding part of the given words
to the beginning letters below them.

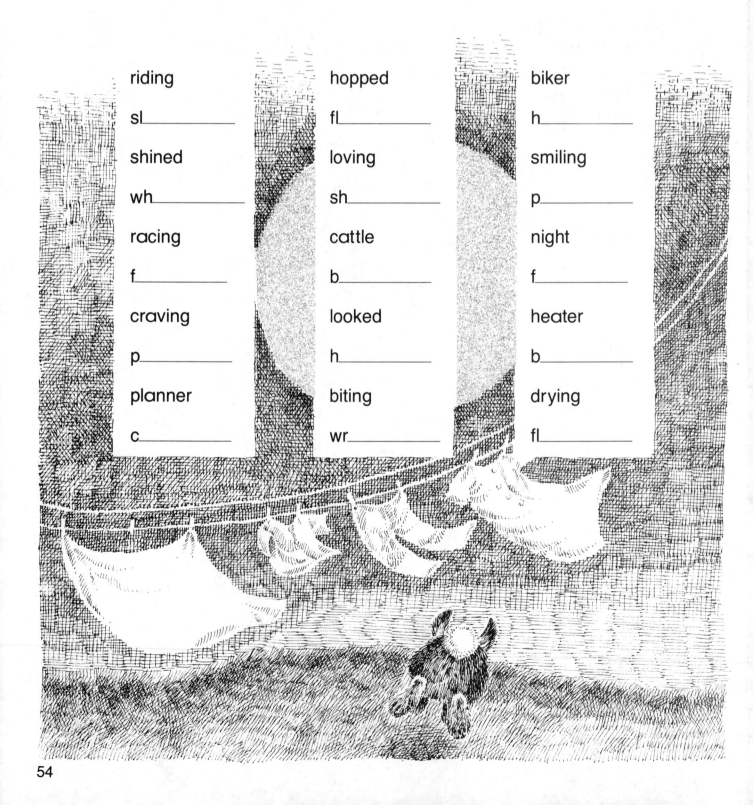

riding

sl_____

shined

wh_____

racing

f_____

craving

p_____

planner

c_____

hopped

fl_____

loving

sh_____

cattle

b_____

looked

h_____

biting

wr_____

biker

h_____

smiling

p_____

night

f_____

heater

b_____

drying

fl_____

April Fool Crossword Puzzle

Sometimes two words try to fool you. They sound the same, but they have different spellings and meanings. Can you find these pairs of words?

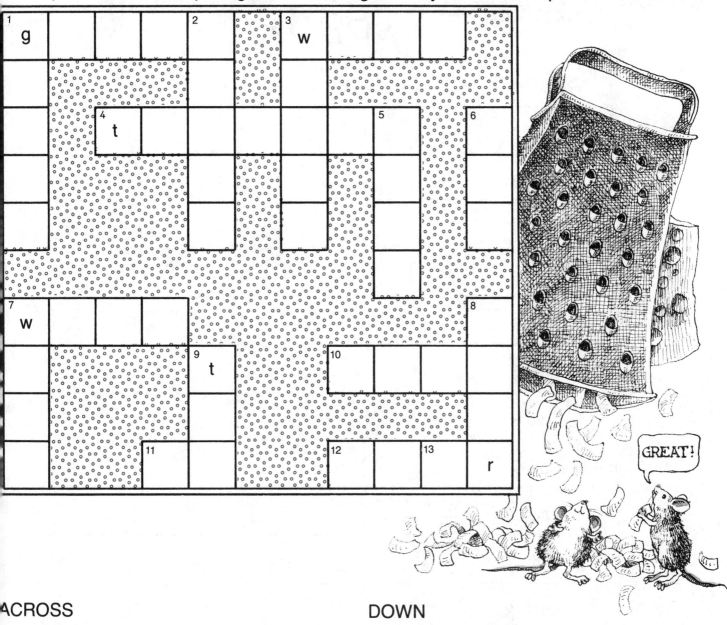

ACROSS

1. Wonderful!
3. Trees are made of this.
4. The ghost went _____ the wall.
7. seven days
10. this place
11. They went ___ the store.
12. two of the same thing
13. a word for self

DOWN

1. a way to cut cheese
2. a word for tossed
3. rhymes with could
5. to listen
6. you use it to see
7. not strong
8. a yellow fruit
9. also

An April Calendar

Write down what happened on each day of April in the story "The April Rabbits."

APRIL

April 1
_____

April 2
_____

April 3
_____

April 4
_____

April 5
_____

April 6
_____

April 7
_____

April 8
_____

April 9
_____

April 10
_____

April 11
_____

April 12
_____

April 13
_____

April 14
_____

April 15
_____

APRIL

April 16 _____

April 17 _____

April 18 _____

April 19 _____

April 20 _____

April 21 _____

April 22 _____

April 23 _____

April 24 _____

April 25 _____

April 26 _____

April 27 _____

April 28 _____

April 29 _____

April 30 _____

You Are Cornered

Print the words that sound the same across and down.

not strong

7 days (down)

w	e	a	k

this place

to listen (down)

to go between

tossed (down)

wonderful

to cut cheese (down)

also

more than one (down)

a yellow fruit

two of a kind (down)

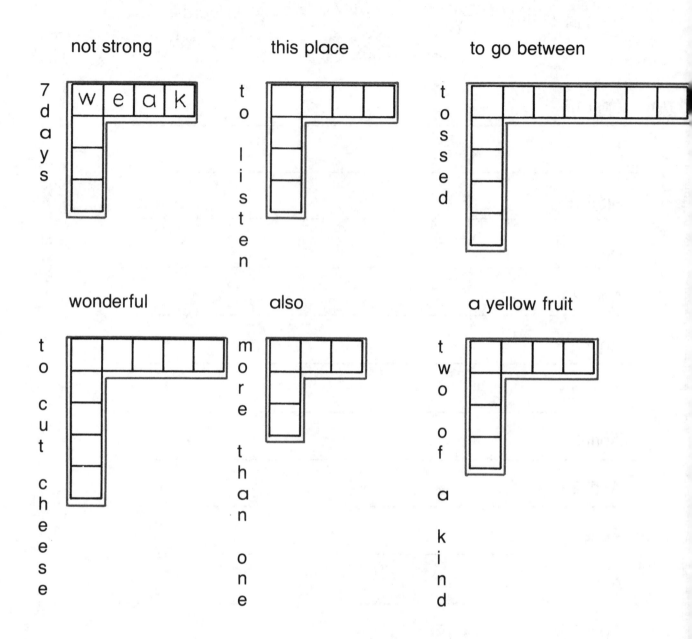

YOU ARE HERE

Covered with Eggs

Write what each person in the story "The Price of Eggs" would tell the judge if there were a trial. Use your own words.

Widow:_____

_____

_____

_____

_____

Neighbour:_____

_____

_____

_____

_____

_____

Stranger:_____

_____

_____

_____

_____

Complete the Thought

These expressions are from "The Price of Eggs."
Can you complete them?

wait and _____

may heaven _____ _____

good day _____ _____

I beg _____ _____

my good _____

too weary to walk _____ _____

tired and _____

take pity _____ _____

he has an honest _____

you have my _____

to make my _____

heaven will _____ _____

happier in your _____

blessed with _____

bitter with _____ _____

to show my _____

count her chickens before _____ _____ _____

Painting Word Pictures

Sometimes, you should add describing words to your sentences
to paint a better "word picture."
Think of some words to describe the following things.
Use your "word picture" in a sentence.

market

_____

spring

_____

street

_____

neighbour

_____

journey

_____

trouble

_____

chicken

_____

judge

Find a Shortcut

Print the short form from column B beside the matching long form in column A.

A   B

she has not _____   he hadn't

I would _____   they're

they will _____   I'll

he is _____   there's

I will _____   they'll

there is _____   he's

I have not _____   I've

he would _____   they'd

I have _____   I haven't

they would _____   he'd

we are _____   we're

it is _____   they've

they are _____   she'll

she will _____   it's

they have _____   I'd

he had not _____   she hasn't

Rain, Rain, Go Away

The poem "Rain" describes a rainstorm on an island in the West Indies.
Use the pattern of "Rain" and your own words to describe
a rainstorm hitting your neighbourhood.

It finally _____

it beat _____

it bounced _____

it banged _____

it rolled _____

it made _____

it spilled _____

it licked _____

it jumped _____

It stayed _____

and then _____

Say It Again

There are many different ways to say the same thing.
Write another way of saying these lines from the poem "Hurricane."

Example:

Big rain coming

There is a bad storm on the way! _____

Neighbours whisper

_____

Dark clouds gather

_____

Gather in the clotheslines

_____

Big wind rising

_____

Branches falling

_____

Raindrops flying

_____

Big wind blowing

_____

Watch Out!

Who said these lines in the story "Why the Tides Ebb and Flow"?

_____ : O Great Spirit, I need a hut.

_____ : Maybe tomorrow.

_____ : Give me a rock to shelter me from the weather.

_____ : Take one.

_____ : Ai-ee! You are sailing too close to the hole in the sea.

_____ : Ai-oo! You are much, much too close
to the hole in the sea.

_____ : Aha! Then I know I am sailing in the right direction.

_____ : That is the rock I want.

_____ : Don't take the rock from the hole in the sea!

_____ : But that's the rock I want!

_____ : I think you are taking the rock from the sea.

_____ : But that's the rock I need.

_____ : Be sure you don't take the rock from the sea!

_____ : But you said I could have it!

_____ : Put back the rock and I will let you borrow it
twice each day.
(So she did!)

NO HUT TODAY

Uh-oh..

The Tides Come and Go

Answer these questions about the story "Why the Tides Ebb and Flow."

When did the old woman live?

_____

_____

Why did the old woman want a hut?

1. _____

2. _____

3. _____

What did the Sky Spirit tell her?

_____

_____

What did Old Woman ask Sky Spirit for the next time?

_____

How did the Old Woman get to the rock?

_____

What warning did Sea Bird give Old Woman?

_____

_____

What warning did Little Silver Fish give Old Woman?

_____

_____

What did busy Sky Spirit say when he saw what was happening?

_____

Why did Old Woman take the rock from the hole in the sea?

_____

_____

What happened when the rock went "fop"?

_____

_____

How did Little Dog try to help?

_____

How did Young Maiden try to help?

_____

How did Young Man try to help?

_____

Did Old Woman put the rock back forever?

_____

_____

What do you think makes the tides ebb and flow?

_____

_____

_____

O What Is That Sound?

There are letters underlined in each of the words in the stewpots.
Under each of those words print the list words that have
the same sound spelled the same way.

boat	toil	blow	sold	annoy	troll	only
floor	hold	coil	joy	post	done	flower
ghost	now	pound	gone	coat	mouse	snow

gr<u>ou</u>nd

c<u>ow</u>

sh<u>ow</u>

r<u>oa</u>d

<u>oi</u>l

t<u>oy</u>

g<u>o</u>ld

m<u>o</u>st

Now and Then

When you write a sentence, you can make it sound like the action is happening now or in the past.
Change each sentence to make it sound like the action happened in the past.

The King is sitting under the palm tree.

_____

The servant is fetching the King's water.

_____

The bird sings near the river.

_____

The Queen is going to see what happened.

_____

The King is getting crosser by the minute.

_____

The Prince listens to the music.

_____

The servant is begging the bird to sing.

_____

The bird keeps his song for himself.

And Then What Happened?

Complete these sentences to retell the story "The Singing Bird."

The King sat _____

He said, _____

Then he said, "Servant, _____

The servant was kneeling down _____

He heard _____

Meanwhile, the King _____

He said, "Wife, _____

She joined in _____

Meanwhile, the King _____

He said, "Son, _____

The Prince joined in _____

The King said, "I _____

He heard _____

He saw _____

_____

He joined in _____

The King thought, _____

The servant _____

The bird _____

The King said, _____

But, the bird _____

The servant said, _____

But, the bird _____

The Queen said, _____

But the bird _____

The Prince said, _____

But the bird _____

Then the servant thought: _____

_____

And the bird _____

_____

Freedom is a special thing,
"Sing, bird, sing!"

Now and Then Words

Sometimes you need words to tell about now.
Sometimes you need words to tell about the past.
Fill in the chart with the missing now and past words.

Now	Past
	caught
bring	
sing	
	shared
know	
say	
	blew
feel	
is	
cry	
	grew
play	
creep	
	kept
	bought
fly	

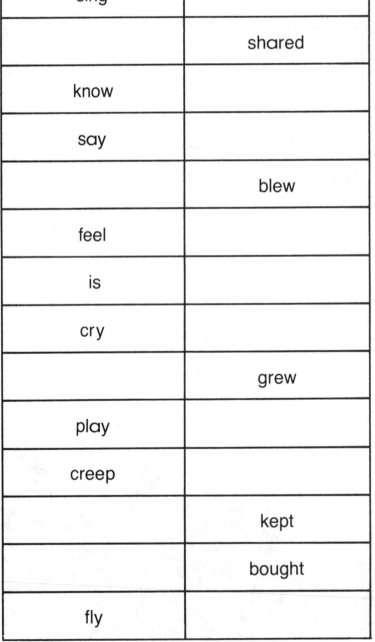

72

What Would Happen If

The poem "If" asks the question "What would happen if?"
Use your own ideas to answer these questions.

What would happen if:

I captured a unicorn in my backyard?

_____

I found a tree that no one had ever heard of?

_____

I could fly like a bird?

_____

I could not speak?

_____

I could stop the rain from falling?

_____

I could talk to birds?

_____

The Duck in Danger

Pretend that you are a reporter for your class newspaper.
Write a news story about what happened to the duck in "Miracle for Maggie."
Don't forget to write a title.

_____

Because, Because, Because

Complete these sentences about the story "Miracle for Maggie."

The duck was lying on the beach because _____

_____

The friends took the duck to Maggie's mother because _____

_____

Maggie's mother put the duck in the sink because _____

_____

Maggie's mother held the duck's head up to feed him because _____

_____

After he was cleaned the duck still could not swim because _____

_____

They shut the duck up safely because _____

_____

The next morning, they put the duck in the bathtub because _____

_____

Maggie's mother sighed because _____

_____

The duck dove and dove because _____

_____

Maggie felt warm all the way home because _____

_____

What Do They Mean?

Explain the meaning of these expressions from the story "Miracle for Maggie."

oil slick _____

Vancouver harbour _____

as limp as Maggie's Raggedy Ann doll _____

_____

half-starved _____

watched wide-eyed _____

laughed with delight _____

natural oil _____

shut him up safely _____

Maggie held her breath. _____

her eyes were worried _____

The bathroom was wet from floor to ceiling. _____

_____

he moved in readiness _____

Maggie was warm all the way home. _____

_____

A Word Search

Circle the words in the puzzle. You should find at least 10.

f	r	i	e	n	d	s	r
e	u	l	p	b	u	n	l
a	z	l	q	f	c	l	a
t	a	s	i	n	k	s	y
h	o	w	t	u	v	o	w
e	s	l	i	q	u	i	d
r	i	m	v	p	y	l	z
s	d	s	t	a	y	u	c

Make a word search puzzle using words from the story.

About Foxes

Use information from "A Narrow Escape" to make your own nature book about foxes.

The Fox in Canada

Description: _____

_____

Name for Young: _____

Name for Female: _____

Where They Live: _____

_____

_____

_____

What They Eat: _____

_____

_____

_____

How They Feed
Their Young: _____

_____

_____

When Male and Female
Live Together: _____

_____

_____

Common Dangers
to Foxes: _____

_____

Problems Foxes
Cause for Humans: _____

_____

_____

What to Do if
You See a Fox: _____

_____

_____

Comparing Foxes

Sometimes comparing a person or thing to something else
helps you to paint a better "word picture." For example,
saying that a person is "as sly as a fox" means that person
is sneaky and clever like a fox.
What do you think these expressions might mean?

as strong as a fox

_____

_____

like a red fox

_____

_____

as quick as a fox

_____

_____

like a hungry fox

_____

_____

hidden like a fox

_____

_____

as wild as a fox after a chicken

_____

_____

What Next?

Print the words in each list in alphabetical order.

blank _____

ball _____

buy _____

best _____

set _____

stair _____

sat _____

sick _____

frost _____

fire _____

free _____

feather _____

table _____

thirsty _____

tell _____

tin _____

cloud _____

citizen _____

cat _____

cent _____

ghost _____

get _____

ground _____

grass _____

List four of your friends' names in alphabetical order.

_____ _____ _____ _____

The Laws of Nature

Use information from the poem "Samuel" and your own ideas
to answer these questions.

Where did the speaker find the salamander?

_____

What is a salamander?

_____

Why was Samuel a good name for a salamander?

_____

Where was Samuel when he died?

_____

How did the speaker feel about Samuel's death?

_____

_____

What law of nature did the speaker break?

_____

_____

What creatures have you removed from their natural homes?

_____

_____

What Kind of Animals?

Write a word to describe each of the animals in the list.

(If your word begins with a, e, i, o, or u, change "a" to "an".)

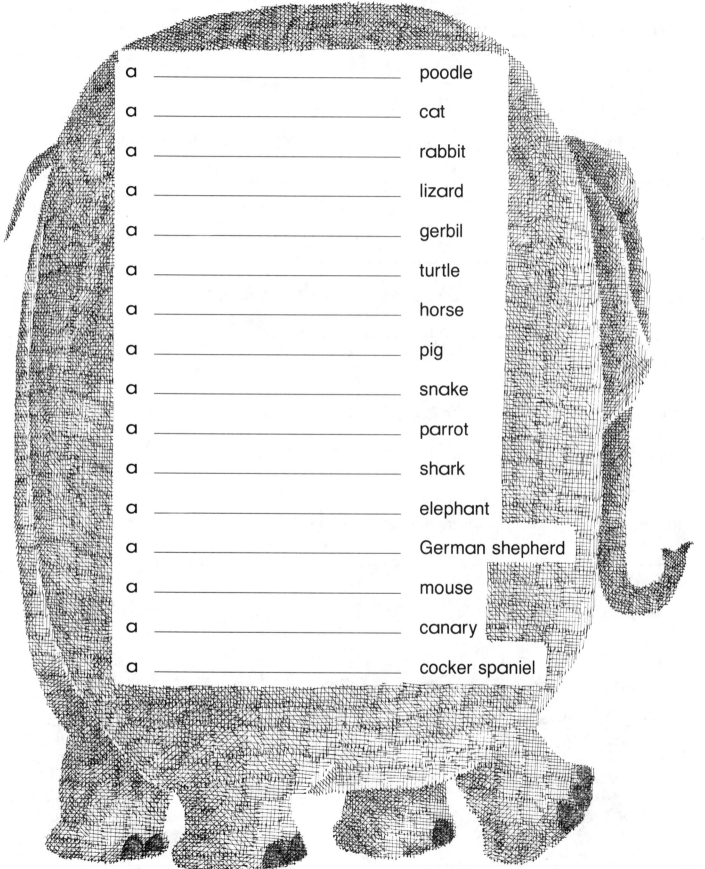

a _____ poodle

a _____ cat

a _____ rabbit

a _____ lizard

a _____ gerbil

a _____ turtle

a _____ horse

a _____ pig

a _____ snake

a _____ parrot

a _____ shark

a _____ elephant

a _____ German shepherd

a _____ mouse

a _____ canary

a _____ cocker spaniel

The Veterinarian's Life

Use information from the story "Doctor Mary's Animals"
and your own ideas to answer these questions.

What kinds of animals has Doctor Mary looked after?

_____

_____

What different things does Doctor Mary do to help the animals get well?

_____

_____

_____

What illnesses have you gone to a doctor to be treated for?

_____

_____

What did the doctor do to help you get well?

_____

_____

How does Doctor Mary prepare for an operation?

_____

_____

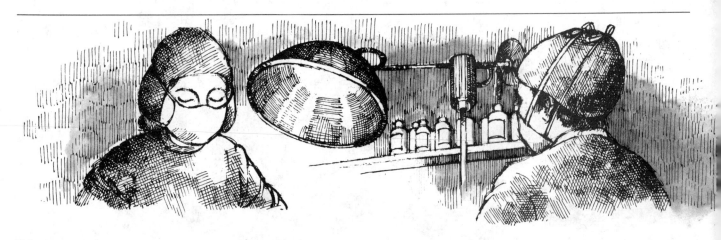

Why do some animals have to stay in Doctor Mary's hospital?

_____

_____

_____

What did Cory think the animal hospital would be like?

_____

_____

How did Cory practise being an animal doctor?

_____

_____

Did Cory get to see an elephant?

_____

_____

Tell about a pet that you or a friend owned that went to a veterinarian.

_____

_____

Would you like to become an animal doctor? Why?

_____

_____

Yesterday, Today and Tomorrow

Change the underlined words in these sentences to make them sound like
the actions are happening at the times given in the brackets.

(today)   Dr. Mary <u>takes care</u> of animals.

(tomorrow) Dr. Mary _____ of animals.

(yesterday) Dr. Mary _____ of animals.

(yesterday) People <u>brought</u> their pets to Dr. Mary.

(today)   People _____ their pets to Dr. Mary.

(tomorrow) People _____ their pets to Dr. Mary.

(tomorrow) Pets and owners <u>will be sitting</u> in the waiting room.

(today)   Pets and owners _____ in the waiting room.

(yesterday) Pets and owners _____ in the waiting room.

(today)   Dr. Mary <u>prepares</u> for the operation carefully.

(tomorrow) Dr. Mary _____ for the operation carefully.

(yesterday) Dr. Mary _____ for the operation carefully.

(yesterday) Dr. Mary <u>gave</u> injections to the animals.

(today)   Dr. Mary _____ injections to the animals.

(tomorrow) Dr. Mary _____ injections to the animals.

A Dog for Company

In the poem "My Dog," the speaker hides behind the sofa with the dog during a thunderstorm. Where could you go with a dog at these times?

You both are hungry and the fridge is empty.

_____

_____

You want some peace and quiet.

_____

_____

You and the dog aren't feeling well.

_____

_____

You both are in trouble.

_____

_____

You have to find two Halloween outfits.

_____

_____

You both need a haircut.

_____

_____

A Bear Driver

Number the sentences in the correct order to retell
the story "A Bumpy Ride for a Bear."

(   )   The bear poked his head out of the barn door.

(   )   We'll go and bang on the back of the barn to scare him.

(   )   My stars, there really is a bear!

(   )   Dad climbed up and started the tractor.

(   )   The tractor took off with a very bewildered bear sitting on it.

(   )   We both raced to the meadow.

(   )   The tractor had hit a small tree in the meadow.

(   )   There's a bear down by the barn.

(   )   You have to know when to stop pretending.

(   )   What are you going to do?

(   )   The bear walked out of the barn and climbed up on the tractor.

(   )   We'll just have to hope the tractor runs out of gas soon.

(   )   I don't think we'll see a bear around here for another twenty years.

(   )   There hasn't been a bear around here for twenty years.

(   )   The bear was stunned but unhurt.

Who's Driving?

Match the sentences with the person who said them in "A Bumpy Ride for a Bear."

I shouted	"Dad! Dad!"
I pleaded	"Get on with your chores!"
I thought	"Mom, there's a bear down by the barn."
I said	"This is too much, Jason."
Dad asked	"Please come down by the barn, Mom."
Dad answered	"He must have believed me after all."
I asked	"The bear must have gone inside the barn."
I called	"Are you still on about that bear?"
He yelled	"My stars!"
Mom scolded	"What are you going to do?"
Dad exclaimed	"There's not much we can do."
Dad cried	"Something has happened."
Dad said	"I don't think we'll see another bear around these parts for another twenty years."

A Bear Hunt

Circle the words in the puzzle. You should find at least 18.

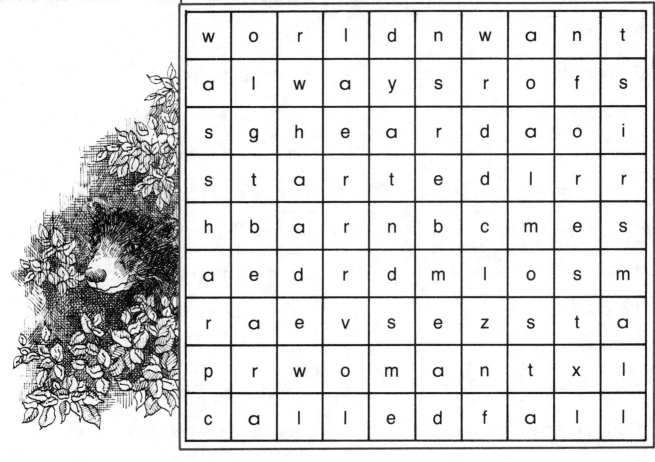

w	o	r	l	d	n	w	a	n	t
a	l	w	a	y	s	r	o	f	s
s	g	h	e	a	r	d	a	o	i
s	t	a	r	t	e	d	l	r	r
h	b	a	r	n	b	c	m	e	s
a	e	d	r	d	m	l	o	s	m
r	a	e	v	s	e	z	s	t	a
p	r	w	o	m	a	n	t	x	l
c	a	l	l	e	d	f	a	l	l

Make a word search using the names of children in the class.

My Word!

Beside each of the words below, print another word that sounds the same, but is spelled differently.

bear _____

hear _____

sea _____

two _____

red _____

tide _____

eye _____

knot _____

be _____

oar _____

aunt _____

through _____

their _____

beet _____

reed _____

heard _____

Why, Why, Why?

Why do you think the characters in "Pooh's Alphabet Book" said these lines?

"It's hard to be brave when you're only a small animal."

Piglet said this because _____

_____

"Long words bother me."

Winnie-the-Pooh said this because _____

_____

"Me having a real birthday?"

Eeyore said this because _____

_____

"I, Winnie-the-Pooh, will find your tail for you."

Winnie-the-Pooh said this because _____

_____

"You're a real friend. Not like some."

Eeyore said this because _____

BEES

(buzzing)

HONEY

"I've got a sort of idea, but I don't suppose it's a very good one."

Winnie-the-Pooh said this because _____

_____

"I just wanted to be sure of you."

Piglet said this because _____

_____

"I suppose, really, I ought to go and see Rabbit."

Winnie-the-Pooh said this because _____

_____

"Well if you listen, Piglet, you'll hear it."

Winnie-the-Pooh said this because _____

_____

"Oh!" said Pooh. "I know."

Winnie-the-Pooh said this because _____

_____   _____

a GRANDFATHER

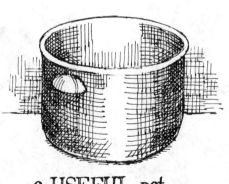

a USEFUL pot
(to keep things in)

An Alphabet Story

Write an alphabet story. The first sentence has to begin with a word that starts with "a". The next sentence has to start with a "b" word. Try to use all the letters of the alphabet.

A_____

B_____

C_____

D_____

E_____

F_____

G_____

H_____

I_____

J_____

K_____

L_____

M_____

N_____

O_____

P_____

Q_____

R_____

S_____

T_____

U_____

V_____

W_____

X_____

Y_____

Z_____

A Letter About Stamps

"Stamp Collecting" was written by a student named Vincent Wong. Imagine that you are Vincent, and write a letter to a pen pal to ask for some new stamps. Use information from "Stamp Collecting" in your letter.

Dear _____

_____

_____

_____

_____

_____

_____

_____

_____

_____

_____

_____

Yours truly,

_____

Stamp Instructions

Stamp collectors must handle stamps carefully because they are delicate.
Write instructions for taking stamps off envelopes and putting them
in an album. You may use the information in "Stamp Collecting."

_____

_____

_____

_____

_____

_____

_____

_____

_____

_____

_____

Stamps of the World

Countries make special stamps for different reasons.
Why do you think they would make these special stamps?

a Terry Fox stamp

_____

_____

an Olympics stamp

_____

_____

a Space Shuttle stamp

_____

_____

an old airplane stamp

_____

_____

a Canadian hero stamp

_____

_____

Stamp Stamp Stamp!

Some words mean "things" sometimes and "actions" at other times.
"Stamp" can mean a thing you put on a letter or an action like marching.

Write sentences using each word two different ways.

drink

(thing) _____

(action) _____

water

(thing) _____

(action) _____

fly

(thing) _____

(action) _____

name

(thing) _____

(action) _____

land

(thing) _____

(action) _____

Building a Word Collection

Underline the part of the word that is the same in each pair of words.
Underneath them print another word with the same group of letters in it.

stamp	earth	new
lamp	heard	threw
r_____	l_____	f_____
hitch	knit	wrap
stitch	know	write
d_____	k_____	w_____
build	ought	walk
builder	thought	chalk
bu_____	b_____	t_____
pour	night	sleigh
four	sight	neighbour
col_____	f_____	h_____

100

Collecting

Divide the collection of words below into four smaller collections.
Print each word in the list where you think it belongs.

bubble gum cards
pen
running shoes
sweat band
thermos
frisbee
crayons

banana
swimsuit
model airplane
jackknife
bubble gum
animal crackers
kleenex

towel
hockey pads
leotards
jigsaw puzzle
chocolate bar
mittens

Lunch Pail

Toy Box

Jacket Pocket

Gym Bag

Sally's Strengths

The story "Sally Can't See" tells about the many things that blind people can learn to do. Make a list of some of the things that Sally has learned to do.

1. _____
2. _____
3. _____
4. _____
5. _____
6. _____
7. _____
8. _____
9. _____
10. _____
11. _____
12. _____

Understanding the Senses

"Sally Can't See" is a story about a girl who does not have the sense of sight. Make four lists of things you think Sally could enjoy by using her other senses.

*Put a star beside one thing in each list that is special to you.

Sense of Touch

_____

_____

_____

_____

Sense of Taste

_____

_____

_____

_____

Sense of Smell

_____

_____

_____

_____

Sense of Hearing

_____

_____

_____

_____

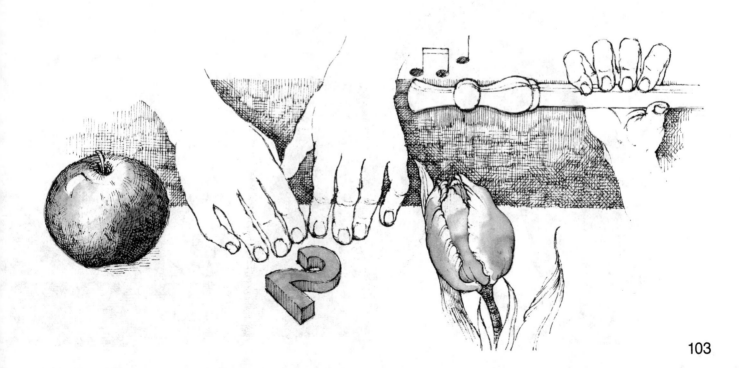

Changing Letters

Before adding a new ending to some words that end in "y",
you have to change the "y" to an "i". Print each of the words
in the lists, using the ending given at the top of the list.

es (more than one)	er (more than)	est (the most)
fly	scary	mighty
flies		
cry	noisy	funny
lady	ugly	silly
baby	pretty	dirty
story	sunny	lovely

	ed (the past)		ly (describing)
carry		happy	
carried			
worry		hungry	
bury		angry	
hurry		noisy	
marry		nasty	
scurry		cheery	

Wishing Wishes

The poem "Wishers" tells you how to make a wish by blowing away
the fluffy dandelion or milkweed seeds.
Write about some other ways of making wishes.

Method 1

_____

_____

_____

Method 2

_____

_____

_____

Method 3

_____

_____

_____

Method 4

_____

_____

_____

What's in a Name?

The beetles in "Meet the Beetles" have interesting names.
Can you guess why they were given those names?

the tiger beetle

_____

_____

the stag beetle

_____

_____

the milkweed leaf beetle

_____

_____

the ground beetle

_____

_____

the flea beetle

_____

_____

the long-horned twig borer beetle

_____

_____

Find the "ee"

The "ee" has been left out of each of the words below.
Print the words adding the "ee"
in the correct place.

btles _____

fr _____

kn _____

mt _____

chse _____

ft _____

bt _____

s _____

frze _____

fl _____

stl _____

whl _____

f _____

hl _____

sht _____

nd _____

The More the Merrier

There are different ways to make words mean more than one.
Print the word that means more than one of each of these under
the correct heading.

beetle	woman	church	hospital	dairy	enemy
mouse	box	splash	mystery	child	candle
country	tooth	chair	favourite	goose	ox
porch	fox	pansy	toad	butterfly	wish

add "s"　　　　add "es"　　　　change "y" to "i"　　a new word
　　　　　　　　　　　　　　　and add "es"

_____　_____　_____　_____

_____　_____　_____　_____

_____　_____　_____　_____

_____　_____　_____　_____

_____　_____　_____　_____

_____　_____　_____　_____

What Does It Look Like?

When you are trying to describe something, it often helps to compare it to something else. For example, you could say:
"A beetle crawling through the grass looks like a tank rolling across a field."

Compare the creatures below to something else.

A grasshopper _____

_____

A bumble bee _____

_____

A mosquito _____

_____

A dragonfly _____

_____

A wasp _____

_____

A hummingbird _____

_____

A garter snake _____

_____

A caterpillar _____

_____

Bugging the Town

Imagine that you are an insect architect. Design a town for bugs.
Include places for bugs to play and have fun, to store food,
and to protect themselves.

Bug City

Architect _____

Listen to Me!

You can add words to sentences to paint better "word pictures."
For example, "a summer afternoon" could be described as
"a steamy, sticky summer afternoon."
Add words to these sentences to describe the things that are underlined.

It was a <u>summer afternoon</u>.

_____

The <u>sand</u> at the beach hurt our feet.

_____

The <u>water</u> made us want to go swimming.

_____

I snacked on a <u>piece of watermelon</u>.

_____

I saw a <u>sailboat</u> coming close to shore.

_____

We had to be careful of the <u>sun</u>.

_____

My favourite food was the <u>strawberry shortcake</u>.

_____

The Tomato Game

There are nine innings in a baseball game. In the story "One Red Tomato," nine things happened before the first tomato turned red.

Number the sentences below in the correct order to tell what happened.

(   ) When the tomatoes had yellow blossoms they were exciting.

(   ) He planted the seeds in thin rows, kneeling on the ground.

(   ) Everyone was waiting for them to turn red.

(   ) Dad dug up a square patch of ground in the backyard.

(   ) Then the blossoms became tiny green fruit and that was more exciting.

(   ) The radishes came first, and then the lettuce, and then the carrots.

(   ) The green fruit got bigger and rounder every day.

(   ) One day, on his way from work, he bought a box of tomato plants.

(   ) Dad bought seeds at the garden shop and read all the instructions.

Mother was standing with her arm around Dad's shoulders and they were gazing down at the first red tomato.

Tomato Questions

Use information from the story "One Red Tomato" and your own ideas to answer these questions.

How long had Dad been the coach of the Pee Wee Royals?

_____

_____

What did the boy mean when he said "Big people get ugly about baseball games."

_____

_____

What was Dad going to do instead of coaching?

_____

_____

Why was Dad's sign "Please Keep Off the Infield" sad?

_____

_____

Why were tomato plants a good choice for a coach's garden?

_____

_____

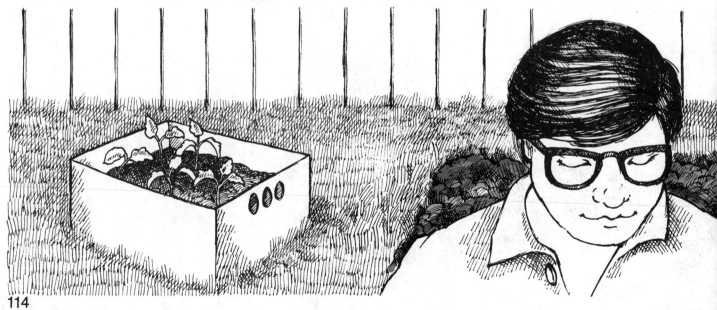

When was Dad's smile "as wide as a slice of melon"?

_____

_____

Why did Dad call Mother out into the garden?

_____

_____

Who did Mother and Dad blame for taking the one red tomato?

_____

_____

What did Dad make to protect the tomatoes?

_____

_____

Why did Dad bat the tomatoes like baseballs?

_____

_____

Do you think the boy ever told his Dad what happened to the one red tomato?

_____

_____

Growing Sentences from Seeds

The sentences on this page are small like seeds in a garden.
You can make them grow by adding words.

Dad coached.

Dad coached _____
                        (whom)

_____, Dad coached _____
           (when)   (whom)

_____, Dad coached _____
           (when)   (whom)

until _____
                        (what happened)

Mother drove.

Mother drove _____
                        (whom)

Mother drove _____ _____
                        (whom)   (where)

_____, Mother drove _____
           (why)   (whom)

_____
           (where)

Dad planted.

_____, Dad planted.
      (when)

_____, Dad planted _____
      (when)   (what)

I ate.

I ate _____
               (what)

_____, I ate _____
      (when)   (what)

_____, I ate _____
      (when)   (what)

_____
              (because)

Dad hit.

Dad hit _____
                (what)

Dad hit _____ _____
                (what)   (because)

_____, Dad hit _____
      (when)   (what)

_____
         (because)

Who Else?

The poet who wrote "Cat" used interesting expressions to describe the movements of the cat. What other creatures could you describe using the same expressions?

yawns _____

opens her jaws _____

shows her claws _____

stretches her legs _____

stands on four long, stiff legs _____

shows her sharp teeth _____

stretches her lip _____

her slice of tongue turns up at the tip _____

arches her back _____

lets herself down with care _____

pads away with her tail in the air _____

Who Are They?

Imagine that you are going to write a story using the same characters that are in "What for You So Crazy?" Make notes about each character to use when you are writing.

Francine: _____

_____

_____

_____

_____

Mr. Livorno: _____

_____

_____

_____

_____

Sample: _____

_____

_____

_____

_____

Another Way to Say

In the story "What for You So Crazy?", people use interesting expressions. Can you think of another way to say the same thing?

"What for you so crazy?"

_____

"stuck on the roof"

_____

"a ball of fur and tiny bones"

_____

"slapping on the paint with a big brush"

_____

"Bello"

_____

"came winging out of the trees"

_____

"Via! Via!"

_____

"crying like a baby"

_____

Yoo Hoo la li, la la, la ley.

"So help me to believe it."

_____

"You stay stuck right there."

_____

"What is this Sample?"

_____

"hugged me until I was squashed"

_____

What are some interesting expressions that your friends or family use?

_____

_____

_____

_____

Ready! Set! Go!

There are many good action words in the story "What for You So Crazy?".
Beside each of these action words from the story, write another word
or group of words that the author could have used instead.

stuck _____

clawed _____

running _____

drives _____

float _____

roared _____

twitching _____

shouted _____

digging _____

took off _____

hopped _____

crawled _____

crouched _____

scat _____

twisted _____

Small, Smaller, Smallest

When you describe something, you can use different word endings to compare it to other things.

Example:

This worm is <u>small</u>.

This worm is <u>smaller</u> than that one.

This worm is the <u>smallest</u> in the garden.

Add "er" and "est" to the words in the list.

small	smaller	smallest
big	_____	_____
tiny	_____	_____
funny	_____	_____
loud	_____	_____
quick	_____	_____
happy	_____	_____
firm	_____	_____
silly	_____	_____
safe	_____	_____

Be careful when you compare things using these words!

good	_____	_____
bad	_____	_____

Describing Singapore

In the story "At Grandmother's House," the author describes
the things he remembers about visiting his grandmother in Singapore.
Write down some of the things he remembers, and then write down
things you remember about visiting a relative or friend of your own.

Grandma:

1. _____

2. _____

3. _____

My relative/friend:

1. _____

2. _____

3. _____

Where grandma lived:

1. _____

2. _____

3. _____

Where my relative/friend lived:

1. _____

2. _____

3. _____

The things they did at Grandma's:

1. _____

2. _____

3. _____

The things we did at my relative's/friend's:

1. _____

2. _____

3. _____

The games they played at Grandma's:

1. _____

2. _____

3. _____

The games we played at my relative's/friend's:

1. _____

2. _____

3. _____

The work they did at Grandma's:

1. _____

2. _____

3. _____

The work we did at my relative's/friend's:

1. _____

2. _____

3. _____

The things they ate at Grandma's:

1. _____

2. _____

3. _____

The things we ate at my relative's/friend's:

1. _____

2. _____

3. _____

Back in the city from Grandma's:

_____

Back at home from my relative's/friend's:

_____

Word Fun

What do you think these words from "At Grandmother's House" mean?

thatched straw roof _____

independence _____

harvesting fruit _____

hair in a bun _____

bamboo baskets _____

curry dishes _____

candied fruit _____

ice ball _____

the ilang-ilang _____

fresh with dew _____

clouds burst like balloons _____

congee _____

swarms of bats _____

bamboo grove _____

mangoes _____

wok _____

My Diary of Important Events

This year many important things happened to you. Think back to each month and write down the most important thing that happened.

September

October

November

December

January

February

March

April

May

June